Original title:
In the Shade of the Philodendron

Copyright © 2025 Creative Arts Management OÜ
All rights reserved.

Author: Adrian Caldwell
ISBN HARDBACK: 978-1-80581-821-2
ISBN PAPERBACK: 978-1-80581-348-4
ISBN EBOOK: 978-1-80581-821-2

Embraced by Nature's Palette

A leafy coat, I wear so well,
Hiding from the sun's loud yell.
My dinner's here, a bug or two,
Just call me nature's BBQ!

Green shades dance, a playful light,
Laughter rings from day to night.
I twist and turn to catch a breeze,
While squirrels plot their cheeky misdeeds.

A Refuge of Tangles and Twists

A wild maze, oh what a sight,
Where plants conspire to take flight.
Vines hold tight, they love to play,
Sometimes I trip, in quite a way!

A spider's web, my nose does catch,
Is that a snack, or just a patch?
I laugh as critters scurry by,
In this green world, I cannot lie!

The Comfort of Lush Canopies

Under poles of leafy green,
I find a seat, like royalty's queen.
The breeze tickles, a playful tease,
My throne of leaves, oh such a breeze!

But wait, what's that? A bird up high,
Is he eyeing me, or passing by?
I wave hello, with playful grace,
In this cozy green, I've found my place.

Echoes of Green Whispers

Whispers rustle through the leaves,
Trading tales of silly thieves.
A curious ant, with tiny flair,
Just marched right in, without a care!

Oh, the songs the branches sing,
Of fallen leaves and frolicking.
A comedy of nature's jest,
Where every day's a feathered fest!

Solace in the Lushness

Beneath the leaves that sway and sway,
I lost my lunch, oh what a day!
A squirrel stole fries, without a care,
In nature's booth, I just sat there.

The vines all giggled, oh what a scene,
A dance-off started, so wild and keen!
I tried to join in, tripped on a root,
The flora laughed, oh what a hoot!

The Poetry of Green Shadows

Where sunbeams scatter, shadows play,
I told a joke, and a flower swayed.
A butterfly sat, rolled its bright eyes,
As I slipped on mud, oh how time flies!

A fern with flair whispered my lines,
Said, "Stick to puns, my friend, no fines!"
With laughter blooming around me bright,
I found my rhythm, oh what a sight!

The Charm of Shaded Comfort

In twilight's giggle, the leaves conspire,
They tease the wind, as I perspire.
A melon slice served by a brave ant,
Declared, "Join the feast, it's quite a plant!"

The air was thick with playful grins,
While rabbits plotted their little spins.
I cracked a smile, they shared a cheer,
Such comical critters, no worries here!

Where Green Dreams Reside

Amid the greens, I dreamed so bold,
Of dancing worms, and tales of old.
They told of battles fought with glee,
While I just watched, sipping my tea.

In clusters packed, the leaves conspire,
A snail on stilts, oh what a flyer!
I burst with laughter; it just can't be,
In this cozy nook, joy's always free.

Where Time Stands Still in Green

Beneath the leaves, a secret dance,
The sun peeks in, but takes a chance.
The cat's chasing shadows, oh what a sight,
While I sip my drink with pure delight.

Lizards on branches, doing a jig,
They're the stars here, bold and big.
The parrot squawks, with comic flair,
Saying things that make folks stare.

A frog on a leaf, drops a beat,
With a leap and a croak, he's quite the treat.
While friends gather 'round, so light and free,
We giggle till dusk, what fun it must be!

As time melts slowly, laughter flies,
Every silly moment, a sweet surprise.
In this green patch, the world can't intrude,
Where joy reigns high, and worries are crude.

The Cradle of Leafy Serenity

Amidst the plants, a world so bright,
A leaf whispers secrets, oh what delight!
Squirrels are plotting their next great heist,
While ants march by, not once enticed.

A hammock swings low between lush trees,
You might hear a snore, or a gentle sneeze.
The breeze is a friend, it tickles your toes,
While butterflies dance in delightful prose.

A gnome in a corner gives a slow nod,
Judging the chaos with a knowing applaud.
The fairy lights flicker with each silly quirk,
As laughter erupts, a blissful perk.

In this cradle of joy, where laughter is king,
Even the silence has its own zing.
So come take a seat, leave worries behind,
In this leafy retreat, hilarity's aligned!

Swaying to Nature's Melody

Bouncing leaves dance with glee,
While squirrels plot mischief spree.
A frog croaks tunes, quite absurd,
As birds join in, a feathery herd.

The wind hums softly, quite a tease,
Plants giggle as they sway with ease.
A butterfly flutters by with flair,
Who's next to trip on nature's dare?

Giggles rise from roots below,
As flowers whisper secrets slow.
Beneath the green, the laughter grows,
Strange friendships bloom where laughter flows.

What a scene, this merry sight,
Where nature dances, pure delight.
So join the fun, don't be shy,
With every sway, we laugh and fly!

Hidden Amongst the Vines

Tangled tangents, oh so sly,
The vines tell tales that make me cry.
A snail dreams big, wishes to race,
While beetles strut with plenty of grace.

In leafy havens, secrets linger,
A gecko's tale, a funny zinger.
Laughter echoes from twig to stem,
As critters gather – who'll win the gem?

Lizards lounge in dappled light,
Throwing shade – a rogue delight.
"Who's the fairest?" the ferns agree,
As they bask and plot endlessly.

Among these vines, the crazy spree,
Where every creature seeks to be free.
"Let's have a party!" one gopher shouts,
While worms wiggle, adorned with clouts!

The Lush Haven's Embrace

In olive tresses, shadows play,
Where lizards bask throughout the day.
The humidity whispers, "Have a drink!"
While bees buzz round in dreams, I think.

A tiny ant carries a crumb,
Thinking it's treasure, all but dumb.
The sun peeks through, a ticklish breeze,
As chattering monkeys swing with ease.

My feet get tangled, oh what fun!
In this green maze, I'm on the run.
"Watch out!" I yell as I trip and spin,
But the vines all laugh, joyfully in.

Dancing shadows, playful tease,
In this haven, feel free to sneeze.
With each whimsy, I chase my fate,
As nature's laughter is just first-rate!

Echoes in the Tropics

The trees are chuckling, what a sight,
As toucans squawk from morning till night.
A sloth moves slow, tries to hula,
While a parrot mimics, "You got the moola!"

Beneath the palms, where secrets hide,
Laughter echoes, a joyful tide.
A beetle's doing the twist with flair,
As frogs provide the rhythm with care.

"Jump, jump," says the frog all bright,
"Splash some water, what pure delight!"
The sun grins down, a playful tease,
As creatures laugh on the warm, soft breeze.

In every corner, the giggles grow,
This tropical dance, a funny show.
Join the frolic, don't wait too long,
Together we'll sing nature's song!

Nature's Breath in the Shaded Grove

Leaves chatter with glee, so sly,
Squirrels plot their next big heist,
Sunlight dances, oh my oh my,
While ants march like they're in a trice.

Beneath the branches, laughter flows,
A chipmunk wears a tiny hat,
The flowers giggle, everyone knows,
Butterflies spin like they're in chat.

A breeze teases, plays hide and seek,
While frogs croak tunes from their lily pads,
Nature's giggles, never meek,
In this shade, no one feels sad.

Oh, what a place of whimsy bright,
Where nature crafts its comical skit,
In the forest, life takes flight,
With every leaf, there's a little bit.

A Postal of Green Memories

In this green realm, odd postcards fly,
A parrot's squawk is a bright hello,
While lizards lounge, no need to try,
They think they're stars in a lively show.

The sun slips through, sending warm rays,
While beetles plan their fancy dance,
Swaying flowers hear nature's plays,
With every breeze, they twirl and prance.

Owls wink from their cozy nook,
As if secrets wrapped in green delight,
While mushrooms gather for a cookbook,
In tropical hush, laughter takes flight.

With every leaf, a memory spins,
As creatures giggle beneath the trees,
Nature's tales and its wild whims,
Create postcards of joy in the breeze.

The Quiet Refuge of Nature

In the hush of green, a light chuckle,
Frogs share jokes, a comedic crew,
Grasshoppers hop, and bushes snuggle,
While squirrels giggle, 'Did you see that view?'

Birds gossip from branches so high,
Condensing tales of the evening sun,
While the leaves sway and sigh,
And nature whispers, 'This is all fun!'

A quick-footed rabbit, he jumps with grace,
Spinning tales of the day gone by,
Every rustle, a comical trace,
As leaves fall, they roll and fly.

In quiet corners, laughter hums,
Where every critter finds a place,
Nature's refuge, no need for drums,
Here, joy glows with every face.

Nourished by Tropical Skies

Beneath the canopies, laughter's reign,
Where mushrooms sprout like silly heads,
Sunbeams tickle in gentle rain,
And vines play 'tag' as fun spreads.

A sloth with shades hangs out so cool,
While iguanas toast under the sun,
Gossiping lizards start a pool,
In the green retreat, life's a pun.

The warm breeze carries giggles and sighs,
As fruits drop jokes and laughter souls,
Chirping crickets harmonize,
With every breeze, the joy unrolls.

Nature's stage, a whimsical spree,
Where every leaf tells tales that tease,
Under the tropical skies, wild and free,
Life's a dance, a joyful breeze.

Underneath Verdant Canopies

Under leafy giants, we play,
While squirrels plot a nut-filled day.
The branches sway and giggle bright,
As we share jokes 'til late at night.

A bird sings tunes of clumsy cheer,
The frogs join in, their croaks sincere.
We dance beneath the shadowed hue,
With nature's quirks, we laugh anew.

Oh, how the sun peeks through with glee,
Tickling toes, as wild as can be.
The flowers smirk, their petals wide,
While bees buzz by, our love applied.

In this realm where laughter grows,
We toast with leaves, as the wind blows.
So cherish fun, where joy persists,
As silly moments bloom like twists!

Whispering Leaves of Silence

The leaves might whisper secrets low,
But we hear giggles in their flow.
"Did you see that?" one vine will say,
"Oops, missed the branch! Let's hide away!"

A lizard strikes a pose with flair,
Sunning right there without a care.
"Look at me!" it nods, so pleased,
As we rejoin, our chuckles released.

And then a moth tries to impress,
By dancing like it's in a dress.
The breeze just laughs at such a sight,
A perfect flier, on a light.

We sway along with vines and boughs,
Sharing laughter that nature endows.
Here in the quiet, we find a spark,
Where humor shines brightly in the dark.

The Secret Grove's Embrace

In the secret grove where shadows play,
We weave our tales, come what may.
With goofy grins and silly stunts,
We find joy in the smallest fronts.

A raccoon trips on its silly toes,
Stumbling, yet never knowing woes.
"Who put that branch right in my path?"
It looks around—oh, the aftermath!

Our laughter echoes in the trees,
While bugs join in, with buzzing pleas.
"Hey, watch this!" we shout with cheer,
As the forest perks up its ear.

Sun bleeds through, like melted gold,
While we spin tales, both brave and bold.
In this embrace of green and fun,
We know well our hearts are one.

Beneath the Green Veil

Beneath the green veil, mischief thrives,
Where laughter blooms and silliness drives.
A butterfly performs a ballet,
While we clap hands, come out to play.

A chipmunk sneezes, a sight so grand,
As we burst forth, ideas unplanned.
"More nuts!" it shouts, with a knowing look,
And hides within its favorite nook.

The shadows dance to our delight,
As goofy moments take their flight.
Nature grins, embracing the show,
In this hidden realm, we steal the glow.

So here we frolic, come take a peek,
In our leafy den, the fun is unique.
With chuckles shared among the leaves,
We craft our tales, as imagination weaves.

Secrets of the Jungle Heart

The monkeys gossip high and low,
While parrots dance in a feathery show.
Leaves eavesdrop on tales so absurd,
As a sloth plays the role of the word nerd.

The iguana thinks he's quite the flirt,
His green scales gleam, but he knows he's a dirt.
Frogs chiming in, all croaks and giggles,
In this leafy lounge, everyone wiggles.

Beneath the Broad Leaves

A gecko strikes a pose, oh so cool,
While ants parade by in a marching school.
A flower whispers secrets to the breeze,
And the vines sway gently, aiming to tease.

The beetles roll dice on the forest floor,
While the butterflies flutter, seeking encore.
Laughter echoes from a hidden nook,
As a snail holds court with tales from a book.

Hushed Conversations of Foliage

The ferns are in on a leafy debate,
Should we let the sun shine or tolerate fate?
Caterpillars giggle, sharing their schemes,
As they plot to munch on the queen's dreams.

A squirrel with acorns thinks he's a king,
While the bees buzz around, making sweet bling.
Whispers rustle through branches so wide,
As the shadows chuckle and gently confide.

The Sanctuary of Verdant Dreams

In a forest café, the critters convene,
Sipping nectar like it's a routine.
The owls order wisdom, "Extra wise, please!"
While the fireflies twinkle like stars with ease.

The raccoon juggles snacks, throws in a flip,
But the bushy-tailed fox just takes a quick dip.
Under broad canopies, jokes come alive,
In this vibrant space, the wild truly thrives.

The Stillness of Leafy Dreams

Beneath the giant leaves so green,
The world feels funny, slightly obscene.
A squirrel in socks, just took a leap,
While ants plan parties, the secrets they keep.

A frog on a throne made of moss,
Himself a king, but he's a total gloss.
Whispers of giggles in shadows collide,
As nature's jesters take their pride.

Beneath the Canopy's Watchful Eyes

A sloth stared down with sleepy intent,
Wondering if today was heaven-sent.
Meanwhile, the lizards dance with glee,
As they play hopscotch on leaves carefree.

A butterfly slips on a dew-drop slide,
And chuckles as it takes a wild ride.
Trees lean in to gossip and tease,
While shadows plot to bring them to knees.

In the Heart of a Leafy Sanctuary

The parrot's loud, a real chatterbox,
And right next door lives a couple of fox.
In leaf-woven chairs, they throw a bash,
With cheeky jokes involving a splash.

A worm in a tie works a desk of dirt,
Claims meetings with sprouts are quite the perk.
Laughter erupts, a whimsical crowd,
As nature's charm serves mischief unbowed.

Tangles of Nature's Serenity

Lianas creep, making a maze,
Where mischievous monkeys spend their days.
A chameleon plays hide-and-seek,
While nearby a raccoon talks to a creek.

A breeze flips hats from one to another,
And leaves spin tales about each other.
The laughter of crickets fills the space,
As everyone joins the leafy embrace.

Nature's Embrace in Silence

Beneath the leaves, the bugs do dance,
Twisting around, a foolish prance.
The sun peeks in, but it's too shy,
While lizards play, and crickets sigh.

A squirrel drops acorns with a thud,
As birds plot mischief, planning their flood.
Frogs croak jokes from their soggy pads,
While nearby plants stand, lookin' mad.

The gentle swish of branches creaks,
While ants march on with tiny tweaks.
Mice gossip softly, tails entwined,
As nature laughs, no worries coughed.

With each soft rustle, a giggle shared,
In this leafy realm, no one is scared.
Rooted and grounded, they share their fate,
A wacky crew, in this green estate.

Harmonies of Leaf and Soil

A worm conducts from beneath the ground,
While leaves whistle tunes, oh what a sound!
The flowers giggle, colors so bright,
While vines hang low, ready for flight.

With every breeze, a chuckle stirs,
As beetles boast of their tiny cars.
The fungi give nods, wise and old,
While daisies laugh at stories told.

Sunlight spills, a golden treat,
As shadows stretch and dance with feet.
A snail in a hurry, got lost in the fray,
Laughs with the toads who don't care anyway.

In this green amphitheater, all join in fun,
Each critter and plant, a part of the pun.
Nature's orchestra plays, no strife in the air,
Creating a symphony beyond compare.

Timeless Stillness in Biomass

Moss feels cozy, snug on the stone,
While ants complain, 'we're all alone!'
The breeze tickles soft, causing a smile,
As nature's hum fills each joking aisle.

Beetles wearing hats, oh what a sight,
Debating the best way to take flight.
Leaves gossip quietly, whispers so sweet,
Trading tales while cruising on heat.

Mice draft plans, plotting a spree,
While frogs laugh loud, 'just let us be!'
The ferns nod, totally in sync,
With laughter drifting in shades of pink.

Each moment a jest, each breath a cheer,
Life's funny chorus, ringing so clear.
In biomass safely, we merrily dwell,
Inside the green giggles, all is well.

Below the Vines, Tales Unfold

Vines twist and twirl, a playful show,
Each leaf tells secrets that nobody knows.
The ground crew rumbles, roots intertwine,
As stories unfold over sips of sunshine.

Under the canopy, shadows grow long,
While mushrooms strum to a silly song.
Chasing around, the butterflies tease,
Dancing on whispers of wanton breeze.

Hiding from peeks of a curious bird,
A turtle starts laughing without a word.
The ladybugs gather, sharing a joke,
While a slow-moving sloth takes a poke.

In this quirky theater, nature's delight,
Each creature's a jester, and all is right.
From roots to the tips, joy softly sways,
Here below the vines, it's fun-filled days.

The Green Treetops' Secret Psalm

High above, the frogs conspire,
In leafy homes, they never tire.
Secrets shared in croaks and hops,
While chatting squirrels take their pops.

Windy whispers float like dreams,
As sunbeams dance in playful streams.
A cheeky bird with quite the view,
Sings out loud, 'Hey, what's to do?'

Beneath the bough, in motley crew,
The critters plot their grand debut.
With acorns stacked and laughter bright,
They scheme for snacks by yellow light.

So if you wander where they play,
Just watch your step and don't delay.
For in this garden, who knows what's true,
A tale of giggles waits for you!

When Sunlight Meets Leafy Veils

Sunbeams tickle leaves so shy,
They giggle softly as they sigh.
A playful breeze pulls off a stunt,
As nature throws a leafy hunt.

In the branches, shadows prance,
The rabbits join in on the dance.
The daisies nod with heads so proud,
While twilight paints the world avowed.

The butterflies, with flair so bright,
Pretend to chase away the light.
Yet in this show of leafy fun,
It's clear the jests have just begun.

With sunlight glints and whispers found,
The canopy brings laughter round.
In this theater, nature plays,
The audience? Just sunny days!

Shaded Whispers of Ancient Roots

Underneath the ancient trees,
A family of ants share ease.
With careful steps, they weave and sway,
Balancing crumbs, come what may.

Nearby, a tortoise takes a peek,
Slowly nodding, yet quite sleek.
'What did you bring from yonder land?'
He muses with a wave of hand.

The roots below, in twisted tales,
Chuckle softly through earthy trails.
They've seen love, mischief, and more,
A timeless book, never a bore.

So if you listen close out here,
You'd catch the laughs that birds hold dear.
In shadows deep, the past unfolds,
With giggles shared, and mischief told.

Encounters in Nature's Courtyard

In nature's court where laughter reigns,
A squirrel juggles with no chains.
The dandelions cheer, so spry,
As busy bees buzz by and fly.

A sudden splash! The frog's a star,
Jumping high, oh, what a czar!
With every leap, he winks and croaks,
Amidst the trees where fun evokes.

The raccoons gather, hats askew,
Planning mischief, just a few.
With shiny eyes and clever schemes,
They laugh out loud at wild dreams.

So wander forth, join in the play,
Where leaves and laughter find their way.
In nature's court, it's never dull,
With all this joy, your heart's so full!

Oasis of Soft-Spoken Flora

A plant named Larry hates the sun,
He wears a hat; he's such good fun.
With leaves that wave like tiny hands,
He throws shade on all his lands.

The cacti laugh; they call him frail,
While snails compete in snail-mail trails.
Together in this leafy race,
They sprout ideas at a slow pace.

On rainy days, they hold a feast,
A gathering that never ceased.
They sip the dew from morning leaves,
And dance around like playful thieves.

So plant yourself in this locale,
Where every leaf gives you a tale.
In this oasis so absurd,
Let laughter bloom; that's the word!

Murmurs of the Tropical Glade

In the forest, whispers flow,
Leaves gossip, 'Did you see that show?'
A parrot tells a joke so sly,
The monkeys snicker from nearby.

Ferns wear hats made out of dew,
They think they're fashionable too.
A sloth in shades takes in the scene,
While geckos gel, quite the green machine.

The wind pipes up with tunes so loud,
It rocks the trees; it's feeling proud.
Even rain joins in the cheer,
It drips a melody we hear.

So if you roam where laughter's grand,
Join leafy friends, make some new plans.
In hidden nooks where joy cascades,
Find merriment in tropical glades!

The Breath of Flourishing Eden

In Eden's heart, the flowers giggle,
Petals twirl; they dance and wiggle.
Roots below plot mischief sweet,
They prank the bugs with ticklish feet.

The butterflies, in fancy dress,
Can't help but cause a bit of stress.
"Who wore it best?" they buzz and flutter,
While flowers laugh, secrets they mutter.

The sunbeams host a silly game,
Of hide-and-seek; it's never tame.
A bloom declares, "I saw the star!"
While daisies claim, "That's just bizarre!"

So in this vibrant, comical place,
Embrace the joy, join the race.
For in this breath of laughter clear,
Every moment brings good cheer!

Veils of Green Serenity

Beneath the veils of verdant hue,
The lizards play peek-a-boo.
With every flip of leafy cloak,
They share their jokes; it's such a hoax.

A toad croaks out a tiny pun,
While fireflies joke about the sun.
The ferns join in with giggles bright,
Creating shadows, pure delight.

In this serene, green tête-à-tête,
The humor grows with every pet.
Plants know well how to engage,
In laughter's dance, they all take stage.

So linger here, in leafy dreams,
Where nature thrives and merriment beams.
In veils of green, let laughter soar,
For joy, dear friend, is never a bore!

Tapestries of Nature's Caress

A vine that tripled in height,
Brought giggles at every sight.
The cat got caught in its twist,
Now he claims he's on a list.

Squirrels hold a daily dance,
In leaves, they prance and prance.
The sun can't find them at all,
They mock it behind a green wall.

The bugs throw a tiny rave,
While ants march like they're brave.
A leaf fell loud as a drum,
Now everybody's feeling glum.

A hawk drops by for a snack,
But the chattering sticks to the track.
"Not today!" the creatures cheer,
As we chuckle with laughter near.

Under the Embrace of Leaves

With every rustle, secrets spread,
The garden gnomes say, "Let's party instead!"
Leprechauns lost their gold and fun,
In this jungle, it's all a pun.

A worm is training for a race,
While butterflies fill the space.
"Ready, set, wiggle!" they shout,
As earthworms start to flout.

The ladybugs gossip non-stop,
"Did you hear who did a flop?"
They share tales of giant ants,
Who think they're still wearing pants.

In shadows deep, a lizard sings,
Hoping to woo the bee with bling.
"Not today, my dear," she said,
"Now buzz off, I've got a thread!"

Lost Among the Ferns

In tangled greens, I lost my way,
A frog croaked out a loud "Hooray!"
He said, "Keep calm and hop about,
The snacks are here; just hear me out!"

A rabbit winks through fronds so thick,
"Get a snack or grab a trick!"
With fern hats on their silly heads,
They plot mischief in secret beds.

The grasshoppers laugh at my shoes,
"Just watch out for the sticky goo!"
They leap and flop with all their might,
As I aim to take flight in fright.

"Excuse me, ferns, which way is home?"
A sloth answers, "In the shade, roam!"
"Thanks a bunch!" I grin with glee,
As I trip over tiny bee.

Secrets of the Green Oasis

In the midst of leaves, secrets thrive,
A prancing snail says, "Stay alive!"
With jazz bands of crickets near,
They play our tune, and we all cheer.

The mushrooms throw a cap parade,
Frogs croon softly, unafraid.
In echoes, they find their beat,
While beetles shuffle their tiny feet.

"Watch out!" a voice squeaks from above,
"A bat is flying, push comes to shove!"
But laughter follows the scary flight,
And everyone stays up all night.

Laughter blooms amid the greens,
Silly antics fuel the scenes.
What bliss it is to linger here,
In nature's jokes, we hold so dear.

Serenade of the Overhanging Green

A leafy hat sits on my head,
I dance around, but hear a spread.
The branches giggle, shake with glee,
'Oh, look at us! We're fancy-free!'

A squirrel laughs as he munches seeds,
While sunlight tickles all his deeds.
The flowers chuckle, petals wide,
'Join us now for the vibrant ride!'

My friends declare, 'It's time for tea!'
But leaves insist on having spree.
So here we sip on nectar sweet,
While nature hosts this merry meet.

Oh, how I love this leafy show,
Where giggles bloom and breezes flow.
With every rustle, life unfolds,
In this green world, where laughter holds.

In the Lap of Flora's Warmth

I found a seat on mossy ground,
Amongst the blooms, I spun around.
A bumblebee tried to steal my snack,
I waved him off with a hearty clack!

The daisies winked and whispered low,
'Hey there, pal, let's put on a show!'
A ladybug giggled, red and spry,
She took the lead, and off we fly!

In this warm lap of nature's flair,
We twirl in petals, without a care.
A grasshopper plays on a trumpet made,
As flowers join in, a grand parade!

So laugh along with this verdant crew,
With every tickle, the joy renews.
In the lap of bloom, with silly cheer,
Life's a dance, and fun is here!

Gentle Strokes of Verdant Shimmers

The leaves do sway as I tell a tale,
Of dancing frogs and a wind-borne sail.
A chorus of chirps joins in the fun,
So vibrant, alive, under the sun!

The ferns nod in delight and mirth,
While bright blossoms boast of their worth.
With a wink, they tease the shy moth,
'Come join us!' they call, with smiles froth.

A gnarly tree burst into a grin,
As I spilled juice of a fruity win.
Bees buzzed by with their busy jest,
Explaining how nature's always best!

The breeze tickles with a playful breeze,
With laughter woven in lush green leaves.
In this magical, shimmering view,
Every leaf laughs, and so will you!

Drifting Through Canopies of Calm

As shadows play in the gentle light,
The plants spin tales from day to night.
An owl looks down, witty and wise,
Says, 'Life's more fun than it appears through eyes!'

A cluster of vines weaves a fine joke,
While butterflies stir the laughter stroke.
The sun sneezes, and leaves all shake,
Raining down sparkles, for goodness' sake!

While I sip on dew from morning's charm,
A lizard darts with a cheeky arm.
He fancies himself in a vegetable race,
But tripped on a root, what a silly face!

With giggles echoing through ferny halls,
Nature's playground, where joy enthralls.
So drift along in this whimsical calm,
Where every moment is a giddy balm!

Secrets Hidden in the Greenery

Under leaves so big and wide,
A hidden world where secrets hide.
Little creatures play and prance,
In their leafy, green expanse.

A squirrel swipes my sandwich here,
While birds gossip without fear.
They mock my hat, so lopsided,
While I just sit here, misguided.

Lizards doing silly dances,
While ants march like they're in a trance.
A jest in nature, oh what fun,
The greenery knows, it's never done.

I chuckle as the branches sway,
Funny how they steal the day.
In a world of green delight,
Life's a joke that's out of sight.

Life in the Shadowy Green

Life sways softly in the shade,
Where plants conspire, plans are laid.
The butterflies flop with great grace,
While ants hold a dance-off race.

Frogs croak like they own the place,
While I sip tea at my slow pace.
The shadows giggle, what a dream,
Life here is one big comic theme.

A chameleon changes just for laughs,
Lost in chat with two green staffs.
They fashion crowns of leaves and twine,
In nature's court, it's truly fine.

Giggles echo through the trees,
While plants join in with the breeze.
Each rustle holds a joke unwound,
In this shadowy delight, laughter's found.

Murmurs of the Tropical Wild

The jungle whispers soft and sweet,
Where laughter drapes in leafy sheet.
Parrots jest with colors bright,
Their chatter spins from day to night.

A wild boar breaks into a trot,
Chasing shadows, laughing a lot.
I can't help but just stand and stare,
As nature's comedy fills the air.

Palm fronds wave a playful cheer,
Shrubs giggle, "Over here, over here!"
Mischief reigns as vines entwine,
Turning dusk to a punchline.

In this tropical maze, we sway,
Becoming jesters, wild and gay.
Each rustling leaf a tale to spin,
In chirps and chuckles, we all win.

Sheltered by Nature's Masterpiece

Beneath the boughs, a comic spell,
A leafy stage where critters dwell.
Frogs recite in croaks and hops,
While fairies stifle giggles, pops!

A tree kookaburra's laughter rings,
While lizards flaunt their newfound bling.
Dancing shadows, what a scene,
In nature's art, we twist and preen.

Mossy cushions for those who nap,
While squirrels play out their acrobatic rap.
The flora chuckles, low and high,
As creatures weave their jokes on the fly.

Under cover of green delight,
Life's a jest from morn till night.
Here, every leaf's a playful tease,
In this masterpiece, we find our ease.

Leaves Like Lullabies

Leaves rustle softly, a gentle cheer,
They hum and they giggle, oh what a dear.
Breezy whispers dance, tickling my nose,
In this leafy choir, anything goes.

Squirrels hold concerts, their acorn guitars,
Crooning to crickets beneath twinkling stars.
Frogs join the fun in their warty blue suits,
Chasing fireflies dressed in bright little boots.

Laughter erupts from the blooms up high,
As daisies debate on how to blush shy.
Petals roll over, with delight they flail,
Trying to keep their gossip a veil.

So here in this jungle, it's never a bore,
A world full of giggles, who could ask for more?
With nature's own humor so rhythmically sweet,
It's a comedy garden where all friends meet.

Whispers of the Plant World

Plants chatter quietly, sipping their tea,
Talking of raindrops and the sun's glee.
Succulents gossip, they roll their green eyes,
About how the cacti wear prickly disguise.

Vines twist and twirl, they're the dancers of fate,
Swinging around branches, never late.
They giggle and shiver at shadows so brave,
In this green soirée, there's no need to save.

A fern tells a tale of a snail's great escape,
While begonias hum in their floral cape.
The breeze plays a tune, plucking melodies sweet,
In a raucous symphony where all roots meet.

So let's laugh with the petals, sway with the grass,
For the plant world whispers, and it's quite the class.
With humor so lush, let our laughter be heard,
In the thrill of the greens, not a word is absurd.

Tranquil Haven of Verdancy

In the calm green nest, where the ferns step light,
Laughter erupts in the soft golden light.
Chatter of critters, a scene so serene,
Creating a world that's fit for a queen.

The daisies play chess with the sun's gentle rays,
While dandelions blow wishes that daze.
The roots tell their stories, the leaves share their dreams,
In this quiet haven, all is as it seems.

A turtle remarks on the sway of the oak,
Telling funny tales, never a joke choke.
With the breeze as the judge, laughter echoes anew,
In a tranquil embrace, where joy's never few.

So linger a while in this place of cheer,
Where humor and blooms brush away every fear.
Life's simply too short not to giggle along,
In a world of green laughter, where we all belong.

Where the Wild Ferns Roam

Ferns frolic gaily under the sun's watch,
Rolling and tumbling, not one to botch.
With winked little eyes, they sprout stories bold,
In the land of the lush, their laughter unfolds.

A mushroom hops along, with a cap so wide,
Cracking up at the ants who march with pride.
They fall in a heap, all giggles and grace,
As mushrooms declare, "We've won this race!"

A wild carrot jolts, in a twist of delight,
Jumping through shadows as day turns to night.
They gather round roots to spin tales of yore,
In this pandemonium, there's always room for more.

So wander with glee where the wild ferns play,
Join in the laughter and let worries sway.
For in their green kingdom, it's clear to see,
Life's a funny game, come play with me!

Shade of Ambrosial Silence

Beneath the leafy drapes we lie,
Sipping lemonade and letting out a sigh.
The world's woes fade like a distant dream,
While I battle ants, plotting schemes.

The lizards gossip, they think they're sly,
While the cicadas hum their lullaby.
I'm glad they can't hear my friend's loud snore,
As we munch on snacks, who could ask for more?

Sunbeams tickle as they peek through leaves,
While nearby, a squirrel steals our peas.
With each crunch, laughter fills the air,
Who knew picnics could turn into a fair?

A picnic blanket turned trampoline,
As we bounce around like we're on a scene.
The shade is nice, but let's be real,
It's the snacks that steal the whole appeal!

A Dance of Petals and Sunbeams

Daisies bow, the sunflowers sway,
As butterflies join in, making their display.
The breeze winks, all the flowers blush,
While bees in tuxedos create a hush.

The petals swirl like dancers at a ball,
Me, tripping over snacks—oh, the fall!
Grass stains on clothes, a trophy I wear,
As I laugh at my mishaps without a care.

Sunbeams zap like confetti in the air,
Each flower whispers, 'Do we really care?'
Nature's comedy, oh what a show,
With every stumble, our laughter does grow.

In this garden's embrace, I find delight,
A party of colors, a pure delight.
Laughter and petals twirl around,
In this grand swirl, joy is truly found!

Enveloped by Nature's Caress

Wrapped in greenery, oh what a sight,
With vines hanging low, it feels just right.
A game of hide and seek with a bee,
Who buzzes around, just too carefree.

My friend trips over roots with a shout,
While I'm doubled over, laughter's about.
The blooms giggle, oh such a riot,
Nature's embrace feels like a quiet diet.

Sipping on smoothies that taste like dreams,
While squirrels sneak bites, plotting their schemes.
The shadows dance; the sun winks bright,
And who knew nature could be so light?

Frogs serenade us with their silly croaks,
As we craft our plans with make-believe hoax.
In this verdant cocoon, we laugh in glee,
A silly tale of silliness, just you and me!

Leaves that Tell Forgotten Tales

Leaves chatter softly, whispers in green,
Secrets of laughter, moments unseen.
A squirrel skips by, carrying a nut,
While I dodge a raindrop that was rather abrupt.

Nature's laughter echoes in the breeze,
As we munch on cookies from a classic tease.
The shadows play games, hiding our snacks,
While giggles erupt from the munching attacks.

In the embrace of shade, we share our dreams,
Competing with frogs, forming funny teams.
With every scratch and itch, we recount old tales,
Of our fanciful adventures and not-so-serious fails.

As the day dances on, sun dips low,
With every lost battle, our friendship does grow.
In this leafy wonder, joy has prevailed,
With each chuckle and giggle, we've set sail!

The Sigh of Leaves in the Breeze

A leaf fell down with a quirky twist,
It whispered jokes that no one missed.
The branches laughed, the vines would sway,
As nature chuckled through the day.

A squirrel slipped on a dewy branch,
And pulled a face that seemed to dance.
The sun peeked in, a curious sprite,
To see the fun in the greenwood light.

A butterfly tripped on a flower's shoe,
Shouted, 'Hey, I've got plans to pursue!'
With pollen flying left and right,
They carried on their airborne flight.

But in the hush at dusk's soft fall,
The leaves just chuckled, oh so small.
With every rustle, they shared a grin,
Nature's humor, just beneath the skin.

Nature's Embrace in Springtime

A bumblebee buzzed with laughter loud,
He wore a hat, oh so proud!
Dancing around in a floral spree,
'Who knew spring had such a degree?'

The daisies giggled at a dandelion's plume,
Said, 'You look like you just left the room!'
While tulips stood tall, striking a pose,
'Fashion week could use some of those!'

A robin hopped with an evening spark,
Said, 'Let's start a band, just after dark!'
The shadows chuckled, joined the sing,
In every nook, joy did spring.

Oh, how the colors laughed and bloomed,
With every petal, spirit resumed.
Nature's embrace was folly set loose,
In every corner, wild and profuse.

Shadows that Sing of Yesterday

Underneath the trees, deep and wide,
Shadows danced like they had pride.
Whispers of stories woven tight,
Giggling shadows in the fading light.

An old cat crept, thinking he'd prowled,
Only to trip on a tree's thick scowl.
"Oh dear," he said, with an awkward grace,
"Next time I'll stick to a safer place!"

A wise old turtle strolled by slow,
Caught a shadow that put on a show.
Brought out a banjo, made it sing,
'This tree knows how to do its thing!'

As night drew near, the laughter grew,
A symphony of whispers that flew.
In the dark, the past would sway,
Lost but found in the shadows' play.

Embraced by the Green Dreamscape

In a garden where mischief does bloom,
Lizards play hide-and-seek, making a room.
A snail wore a shell that glittered bright,
Claimed it was perfect for the moonlight.

The daisies held meetings for style designs,
While violets plotted to steal some vines.
"Oh darling," they said, "our splendor's no chance!
Let's twirl and sway in a fashion dance!"

Giggling frogs played a tune with their croaks,
Bouncing on lily pads, laughter evokes.
The wind took part, swirling the fun,
In the heart of the garden, joy had begun.

But as twilight settled, dreams took flight,
The plants whispered secrets in the night.
In this green world, delightful and free,
Life was a joke, and nature's the key.

The Quietude of the Canopy

Beneath the leaves, a squirrel naps,
While ants parade with tiny traps.
A lizard yawns, sun-soaked and bold,
Exchanging tales of warmth and cold.

Birds chirp gossip, pure amusement,
While crickets hum in their own tune.
A fluffy cat creeps, tail like a whip,
Ready to pounce, but takes a trip.

Nature's laughs, a symphony,
In leafy shades, the world's a spree.
The rustling wind, a secret tease,
Where every critter's prone to sneeze.

A hammock swings with whispers light,
As dappled beams dance, pure delight.
Here we laugh beneath the green,
In this quirky scene, oh so serene.

The Secret Garden's Respite

In a hidden plot where onions grow,
Bumblebees float, putting on a show.
A gnome stands guard with a crooked grin,
Not sure if he's lost or just in sin.

Zucchini vines stretch, a leafy maze,
While beetles plot their sneaky ways.
The garden hose, a serpent's smile,
Sprays the dog, who shakes in style.

Sunflowers dance, their necks out wide,
Laughing at clouds that roll and slide.
A kooky crow caws, with flair in stride,
This delightful chaos, where joy can't hide.

In corners lush, the fruits conspire,
To lure the taste buds, fuel desire.
With laughter bubbling like the broth,
A garden's whimsy, never doth sloth.

Dappled Light and Gentle Shadows

Sunbeams filter through the leaves,
Painting patterns, watch how they weave.
A playful breeze skips through the vines,
Tickling noses, crossing the lines.

A chubby raccoon stumbles, slips,
Chasing a butterfly, oh what a trip!
While frogs in chorus croak their plans,
To throw a party with tiny fans.

Twinkling stars in daylight's glow,
Whisper to flowers how much they know.
A beetle dons a tiny hat,
While ants insist, they've seen that cat.

In this lush haven, giggles reign,
Nature's humor, free of strain.
Join the antics, lose your frown,
In these shadows, we own the crown.

Life Beneath the Green Arch

Under the arch where ferns sway low,
A dance unfolds, weird and slow.
With frogs that wear spectacles quite chic,
And turtles that ponder, "Am I unique?"

A hedgehog rolls, seeking the sun,
Revealing all he thinks is fun.
While tiny snails take their sweet time,
Plotting world domination—how sublime!

Flowers gossip 'neath the trees,
Swapping stories on the breeze.
A buzzing bee, with no sense of care,
Mistakes a shoe for a bloom, how rare!

So here we lounge, the laughter free,
Amidst this wacky, wild jubilee.
Beneath the green, the humor scrawls,
In this leafy world, joy never stalls.

Lush Shadows and Dreamy Echoes

Beneath the leafy canopy tight,
Tiny critters play in delight.
They dance and prance without a care,
Whispering secrets in warm air.

A squirrel debates a big leaf hat,
While a lizard mocks the fluffy cat.
The sun peeks in with a cheeky wink,
As nature's laughter begins to sync.

A butterfly struts in vibrant hues,
Tickling the breeze with fancy moves.
Chasing dreams with every flap,
In this garden of giggles and naps.

Here mischief hides in every nook,
A playful tune in every crook.
So sip your drink, and take it slow,
In this joyful shade where smiles grow.

The Gentle Tickle of Tendrils

Vines twist and curl in a merry spree,
Giggling leaves whisper, 'Come play with me!'
A playful breeze ruffles my hair,
As I'm caught in this verdant snare.

A pesky parrot has much to say,
Reciting jokes to brighten the day.
With every squawk, a punchline lands,
In this leafy realm, humor expands.

In the corner, a frog makes a leap,
Into a puddle with a splash so deep.
The audience laughs, their ribbits in cheer,
Celebrating joy for all gathered here.

So let's raise a cup, toast to the fun,
Underneath the green where laughter's spun.
In this jungle of joy, we'll dance and play,
Finding humor in life's colorful display.

Serenity Beneath the Boughs

A hammock sways, oh what a sight,
Where dreams tickle paws through the night.
A chipmunk hums a lullaby tune,
While the stars drop down like vibrant balloons.

Tangled branches embrace the light,
A mood so merry, spirits take flight.
A caterpillar starts a debate,
On who's the prettiest, it's hard to relate!

The gentle rustle forms a band,
Leaves applaud with a clapping hand.
As butterflies play hide and seek,
In this serene nook, they all get cheek.

Relax and chuckle, let worries cease,
Under this canopy of leafy peace.
Nature's stage hosts a quirky show,
Where giggles and joy are free to flow.

A Tapestry of Green Reflections

A vivid quilt of leaves unfurls,
While munching bugs twirl and swirl.
They share faint laughs, a tiny feast,
As shadows grow and joy's released.

A curious snail ponders the day,
While a wise old tree watches play.
Tickling tendrils tease the air,
In this green tapestry, humor's laid bare.

Bright blooms giggle as bees arrive,
Crafting chaos where spirits thrive.
Nature's jesters in a playful spin,
Weaving laughter as breezes begin.

So rest awhile, take in the scenes,
In this leafy wonderland of greens.
A playful heart is what we seek,
For nature shares joy each day of the week.

Dancing Shadows of the Tropics

Under the leaves, just take a peek,
Lizards prance, so sly and sleek.
The sun can't find the path to creep,
While crickets chirp and secrets keep.

A parrot squawks a joke or two,
Mocking the toucan's silly hue.
Palm fronds wave as if to say,
'This is the most fun way to play!'

With every rustle in the breeze,
Dancing shadows, if you please.
A hammock hangs just right for naps,
But first, let's dance with all our chaps!

So come along, don't be so shy,
Join the ecosphere, give it a try.
Among the vines, we leap and twirl,
In nature's circus, life's a whirl.

Where the Foliage Breathes

The plants all gossip, oh what a crew,
Rumor has it, they saw you too!
With every leaf a waving hand,
Come join the fun in this leafy land.

Blades of grass have quite the sass,
Telling tales of who's first and last.
The winds can't help but chuckle and blow,
As vines twist up in a green tango.

A sunflower winks, what a flirt!
While daisies giggle in their skirt.
The sunbeams giggling all around,
In this garden, joy is found.

If plants could laugh, oh what a sound,
In this jungle, laughter knows no bound.
Join the party, don't be late,
Where the foliage breathes, we celebrate!

The Quiet Dance of Leaves

Leaves that shimmy, oh so sly,
With a whisper, they say hi.
Each petal joins in on the fun,
Dancing gently, one by one.

The breeze brings laughter on its way,
While shadows play a child's cabaret.
Nature's rascals, what a sight,
Twisting, swirling, pure delight!

When the sun sets, the giggles fade,
Yet the moonlight brings a masquerade.
Silhouettes twirl, a merry crowd,
In the silence, they're still loud.

So grab a leaf and give it a spin,
Join in the laughter, let the night begin.
You'll find that joy is all around,
In the quiet dance of leaves, it's sound!

Hushed Moments Among the Vines

Vines are tangled, what a mess,
Yet in this chaos, we find success.
With every twist, there's a giggle anew,
Nature's playground, just for you.

Behind each leaf, a secret is shared,
With a wink and a nudge, they are all prepared.
A critter hops, its dance quite bold,
In this jungle, laughter never gets old.

The sun peeks through with a cheeky grin,
Playing hide and seek, where do we begin?
Among the vines, with whispers and laughs,
Time slips away, the moment halves.

So come unwind, let worries release,
In this leafy haven, find your peace.
With hushed moments, laughter will bind,
In a world of greens, joy is designed.

The Allure of Hidden Green Spaces

Beneath the leafy blanket lies,
A world of mischief, sweet surprise.
A squirrel dances, quite the show,
While birds plot schemes, you'd never know.

The plants conspire, a leafy team,
In the garden, nothing's as it seems.
A butterfly in shades of blue,
Flirts with the flowers, oh so true.

Toads play cards beneath the oak,
While laughing leaves, they softly spoke.
The secrets held in every nook,
Would make a storybook, oh look!

So when you wander, take a peek,
For hidden fun is what you seek.
In every corner, life is bold,
A green adventure, yet untold.

Nature's Quiet Muse.

A lazy lizard on a rock,
Snoozes 'neath the ticking clock.
With sunlit dreams and leafy sighs,
He dreams of cake and sunny pies.

The ants parade upon their trail,
Shuffling snacks, they never fail.
They trade the crumbs like stock market shares,
While checkout frogs give quizzical glares.

Breezes giggle through the trees,
Tickling branches with playful ease.
And when a raindrop hits the ground,
It's just the earth's way to rebound.

So let your heart be light and free,
Like nature's quirks, oh can't you see?
Creativity thrives in the trees,
Where humor blooms with every breeze.

Under Leafy Canopies

A critter swings from vine to vine,
With style that's simply so divine.
His friends below, they cheer and shout,
"Swing it high! Don't fall down, or pout!"

The mushrooms giggle, round and stout,
They host a party, no doubt about.
With tiny hats and little shoes,
They dance and laugh without a snooze.

Grasshoppers tune their tiny strings,
A concert pops beneath the wings.
And crickets chirp a lullaby,
As glowing beetles zip on by.

So find the joy where green things dwell,
In quirky tales they like to tell.
With nature's laughter all around,
In leafy realms, joy can be found.

Whispering Green Embrace

Where green ghosts tease and tickle feet,
Among the ferns, we skip and meet.
A hedgehog holds a grumpy face,
As if to say, "This is my space!"

Caterpillars plot a great escape,
While worms debate their curvy shape.
The flowers gossip, every hue,
"Did you see what that bee just blew?"

A breeze reports the latest tale,
Of cheeky critters in the vale.
While trees shake hands with all their boughs,
In this lush court, a welcome pause.

So laugh with life as nature plays,
In whispering green, let's spend our days.
For every giggle, every glance,
Turns quiet moments into dance.

Veiled in Nature's Grace

A critter crawls with wiggly grace,
While leaves above play hide-and-seek.
A dance of vines, a leafy chase,
Oh, watch the squirrels! They're quite unique.

Among the plants, a laugh we hear,
A polka of flowers, a cheeky show.
The wind joins in, it's quite unclear,
Is that a gust or a friendly blow?

Beneath the greens, they form a band,
The bugs all chirp in perfect tune.
With every step, the petals stand,
To cheer our feet from noon to moon.

A throne of leaves, where joy is held,
And nature's jesters prance around.
Here laughter blooms, and pranks are swelled,
In gardens where the fun is found.

Dancing with Shadows of Leaves

When shadows flirt with noon so bright,
I trip over roots, oh what a sight!
The ferns all giggle, their fronds a-blush,
As I tumble down with quite a rush.

A dance-off starts, oh what a game,
The vines sway low, encouraging fame.
I strut my stuff, oh how I twirl,
The petals clap, giving me a whirl.

But wait! What's that? A bee in flight,
With all my moves, I'm quite the fright!
Buzzing around, it claims the stage,
I step aside, evaluate my age.

In leafy arms, I seek my rest,
A laughter track, oh what a jest.
Surrounded by greens, I smile wide,
In this merry dance, I take my pride.

The Sanctuary of Lush Thoughts

A quiet nook where whimsy sparks,
With chatter of frogs and snappy larks.
Leaves take notes of silly dreams,
As sunbeams jest and sunlight beams.

Under the gaze of a curious fern,
I scribble jokes, oh how they churn!
Doodles of gnomes in a silly race,
All hiding away without a trace.

The flowers gossip, whisper too,
About the snail, it's quite the crew.
I crack a smile, in this green space,
Where laughter thrives, and time's a race.

My thoughts take flight on the breeze so light,
The ants parade in their fancy rite.
In nature's hall, with giggles unfurled,
Inventing a joke, that's how it's twirled.

Cloaked by Ferns and Blossoms

Behind the fronds, a puppet show,
With roly-poly bugs putting on a glow.
The daisies giggle, the violets swoon,
As ants tap dance to a merry tune.

Tangled in laughter, bushes all sway,
The bees have joined, what a grand display!
A comical drama unfolds in green,
With every twist, it's quite the scene.

I sit and chuckle, beneath the trees,
While grasshoppers leap with amusing ease.
A flower pokes me, "Hey, join the fun!"
So I sway along, under the sun.

Each leaf a character, every shade a laugh,
In this tangled world, it's a comic path.
With nature's jesters, the humor grows,
Cloaked by blooms, in glee, it flows.

www.ingramcontent.com/pod-product-compliance
Lightning Source LLC
Chambersburg PA
CBHW070319120526
44590CB00017B/2739